Other books by Author

WW I   The Battle Of The MInd
WW II   This My Cell
WW III   Scars And Memories
WW IV   Voices
WW V   Alone I Roam
WW VI   2020 Deepend
WW VII   Seven
WW VIII   My Mental State

... more will be revealed soon...

WAR WITHIN

WW III:
SCARS AND MEMORIES

VOLUME 3 OF 7

MICHAEL R. BANE

WESTBOW
PRESS®
A DIVISION OF THOMAS NELSON
& ZONDERVAN

WestBow Press books may be ordered through booksellers or by contacting:

WestBow Press
A Division of Thomas Nelson & Zondervan
1663 Liberty Drive
Bloomington, IN 47403
www.westbowpress.com
844-714-3454

All Scripture quotations are taken from the King James Version.

ISBN: 978-1-6642-3522-9 (sc)
ISBN: 978-1-6642-3523-6 (e)

Print information available on the last page.

WestBow Press rev. date: 06/18/2021

CONTENTS

Chapter 1 Seeds

Chapter 2 Promises

Chapter 3 Death

Chapter 4   Life

Chapter 5   Faith

Chapter 6   Hope

Chapter 7   I Became We

DEDICATION

Scars and Memories

This may seem generic, but I choose to dedicate WW3 to you. The one who shares in the struggle, and the victory. This journey, this life is not easy, but it is simple. Yesterday is gone; tomorrow is not promised. All we truly have is today. It is a gift from God. What I do with today, this moment is who I am. My past cannot define me, or you. So lets make some good choices today. Lets love ourselves, and others. Only then, can we accept love. You are so worth good things. "Peace"

INTRO WW 3

Scars and Memories

So as I think about WW 3, Scars, and Memories. The thought came to me that not all scars are painful, and not all memories are good. But each one did have a play on what I have became. I could not be me without each one. The good, the bad, and the ugly. They are all pertinent to who I am. And honestly I would not change, or try to escape any of them. For they are the past. I hope you can relate.

Also a very important revelation, is that we are more alike than we are different. I am no longer alone. Neither are you ....

CHAPTER 1

SEEDS

Matthew 13:8, 9

But other fell into good ground, and
brought forth fruit, some an hundred fold,
some sixty fold, some thirty fold.
Who hath ears to hear, let him hear.

KJV

WHEN IT WAS WRITTEN

I PLANTED SOME SEED

I looked out my window, and what
did I see?
My first inclination was just
another dead tree.
I looked and I pondered, and
I asked myself why.
If I didn't change my outlook,
I knew I would cry.
My love, and my patience
I knew, it did need.
So I went to that spot
and I planted some seed.
Then one day when I was
Feeling so low, and in doubt,
I noticed my seeds
were beginning to sprout.

I really felt proud for this
thing I had done.
But I remember God brought
the rain, and the sun.
This is more than a story
or a ryme of a tree.
What I thought was my window
was a mirror you see.
Those new trees
were all of you,
and that dead tree was me ...

MY PLANT

I noticed my plant
reaching for the light.
The leaves that were dying
now looked bright

What started with two
is now maybe twenty
God gives so much
and I give it plenty

Brought by an Eagle
and now it did soar
my plant is my own
God, and I made it grow

From soil, to root
to the tip of the vine
my plant in my window
it truly is fine.

EACH TIME

Each time we succeed at a small task
we must thank God for the ability.
For when we remember Him, He remembers us.
After all everything we have, comes from Him.
His strength we find from deep within.
And each time we love, we share a
piece of Him
Shared love grows.
It can not be stored up in barns.
It must be used.
And each time we learn something new of Him
we must share it with others.
Wisdom, and knowledge they are key
For when we share a piece of Him
that we learned
He remembers us each time,
and gives us more
and in turn we can give more.
More love.
And all love comes from Him ...

FAMILY TREE

I tried to do my family tree
each limb was broken it did seem
branches full of broken dreams
Why did it have to continue through me?
Why couldn't I stop?
Why couldn't I see?
The leaves were rotten
Whats it mean?
The roots were full of death, and disease
It was a family curse, it seems.
Broken promises, broken dreams.
And of course,
it didn't stop with me.

I passed it to my daughter Cheré.
When does it stop?
When does it cease?
And now I know its up to me
to stop this curse
to stop this thing.
To grow new fruit,
to plant new seeds.
To change this thing, my family tree.
So now I know, its up to me!!!

YOUR GARDEN

What is in your garden?
How does your garden grow?
Do you realize you reap?
Of that of which you sow?
Are your plants speratic?
Or are they lined neat in a row?

What is in your garden?
Is it overrun with weeds?
Or does it produce good fruit?
Did you plant new seeds?
And do you realize it God?
Who supplies all your needs?

What is in your garden?
What is it that you've grown?
Did you plant your seeds good & deep?
Or were they simply thrown?
Is it just another garden?
Or did you make it your own?

NEW LIFE BEGINS

Spring is now here
and new life begins
the cold of winter, and
the death it brings is gone.
As color returns to earth
so does hope.
The gentle rains wash death away
and new life begins.
So as the seasons change
so do I.
Change is not always comfortable
but it is necessary
things can not stay as they are.
Spring is now here
and new life begins.
The sun warms the air
and also my heart.
God is in control.
And I find comfort
with comfort comes peace
and new life begins.

CHAPTER 2

PROMISES

Hebrews 10:23

Let us hold fast the profession of our faith
without waivering. For He is faithful that promised.

KJV

WHEN IT WAS WRITTEN

BROKEN PROMISES

Broken promises, they can cut deep
years later, I still can't sleep
so many promises, I did not keep
I watched you cry, I watched you weep

Broken promises again, and again
I told you we'd go, but I never said when
I said I'd be an hour, it ended up ten
the lies that I told, when you asked where I'd been

Broken promises, broken dreams
I broke your heart, it truly seems
the things you heard, the things you seen
I became hateful, I became mean

Broken promises, the numbers are vast
I can't change it now, their in the past
It may take time, it won't come fast
But I ask your forgiveness, sincerely at last.

TOMORROW

Nobody is promised tomorrow
each breath of air brings life
each moment is precious
each day is a gift
tomorrow may never come
God breaths life in me
Moment to moment I live
day by day I am
hope is in tomorrow
today is all I truly have
nobody is promised tomorrow
I must live life today
I can give, and receive love today
but portions are only for today
each day needs to be replenished
today is all I truly have
nobody is promised tomorrow

ALL WILL BE WELL

All will be well
when I stay on the path
and believe, and know
without a shadow of a doubt
that God is with me
All will be well
when I help another
along his journey
and not be selfish
but to think of his needs
All will be well
when I remember
who I am
and whose I am
and when I share this love with others
All will be well
God will never give me,
more than I can carry
when I help you carry your load
mine becomes lighter
and without a shadow of a doubt
all will be well

BLESSED REDEMPTION

Blessed redemption
Forgiveness and love
It came from Jesus
It came from His blood

He is my Savior
He is my Lord
When He went to calvery
And was nailed to that board

Blessed redemption
Now I am free
It came from Jesus
He did it for me

He is my Savior
He is my Lord
Blessed redemption
For that I am sure ...

THE MORNING

When I rise in the morning
and I get out of bed
and I thank God that I'm not dead
I realize what you said
and the gratitude, there's no dread
I start my day in prayer instead
and know that by God's spirit, I'm led
and thank him for another day, my bread
my salvation through Jesus, He bled
when I rise in the morning
and I get out of bed
and thank God that I'm not dead
and the gratitude, there's no dread
when I rise in the morning
there's hope instead
But I must pause, and check my head ...

"VS"

A method to my madness
where do I belong?
As I trudge along this journey
and realize I'm not alone
If I pause, and search
within, throughout
and my spirit awakes
the madness, turns to peace
and true knowledge
is to accept that
it is not of my doing
God is the peace-maker
and knowledge turns to wisdom
where I've come from
and what I've seen
is not as important
as who I am now
and whose I am always
and whose will I do
mine or His
to choose
peace, or madness

CHAPTER 3

DEATH

Romans 6:4a

Therefore we are buried with him
by baptism into death.

KJV

WHEN IT WAS WRITTEN

DEATHS DOOR

Death tried to suffocate me
I could no longer breathe
I took one last breath
and said enough
I want to live
and now I must choose to live
I must change my ways
now I can breathe
I can see past deaths door
and I truly live
it is my choice
and today I choose to live ...

MURDER NOW

Will you be the death of me?
I look at you
But you are not what I see.
Murder now, is that
What will be?

Why will you be the
death of me?
Murder now, is what I see
I look at you, and
wonder what will be –

Will I allow you to
be the death of me?
Murder now, it will not be
I look at you, and
its you, I see –

SYSTEM DOWN

System down, I need some power
my heart is black, and
my soul is sour

It feels like this might be
the twelfth hour

The bell tolls, internal
time is not time now
time is eternal

The tables are turned
full revearsal

System down
we have a problem
with no solution

My heart is black
my soul is sour

– internal desolation –

SCREAMS

When you ask me how I feel
and all I say is numb
its hard for me to express myself
the depths from where I've came
my mind screams, I am insane
See me now, what I became
my heart is cold, my soul is stained
and as I open up my mind
manic chaos is what I find
life is full, but death is near
when I close my eyes the screams I hear
How much more can I bare?
To learn to love, and learn to care
and silence the screams within my head
now its time to love instead.

DEATH

When I feel my heart flutter
and I know that death
is only one breath away
I try to hold on to life, and not let go
when my spirit is left empty
a dark, lonely hole
I try to hold on, and not let go
when my minds eye sees nothing
but evil, and I search deep
but find no love
my life is but a moment
and I find peace in the fact
that death is near.
So now, I close my eyes forever
there, is no more pain, death has won
and now my new life begins,
For my spirit lives forever
and death can no longer scare me
so that now I truly live.

SIN AND LIES

Nothing hurts worse than
sin and lies ...

The demons snickers
as the angel flies ...

Life is over for the old man
he dies ...

And new life begins
as the new baby cries ...

But nothing hurts worse than
sin and lies ...

IN MY HEAD

Guess how I'm feeling in my head?
No more fear, no more dread
I'm still alive, I should be dead
the things I've done
the things I said
Its all still alive in my head.
Remembering all the things you said
I felt you grow
the pain you fed
confusion, now its calm instead
I was alone, my heart it bled
I'm still alive
You want me dead.
Now there peace, in my head.

DEAD MAN DIES

When a blind man cries
and the tears
stream from his eyes
He can not see
your reaction
or if you are near
you must take his hand
and dry his face.
When a dead man dies
and there is no one there
He still dies
and He is gone forever
so how can a
dead man die?
He is not truly alive
If he has no love to give
these may be my mission
this may be my life
when a blind man cries
and when a dead man dies ...

CHAPTER 4

LIFE

Romans 6:4a

That like Christ was raised up from the dead
by the glory of the Father.
Even so we should walk in newness of life.

KJV

WHEN IT WAS WRITTEN

LIFE DOESN'T HAVE TO HURT

Why does life hurt so much?
It doesn't have to be this way.
a kind word
a gentle touch
The choice of what we do, and say
to make the difference in someone's life
to pass out love, instead of strife
a kind word
a gentle touch
expecting nothing in return
it doesn't have to sting, or burn ..
where there is a will, there is a way
to put a smile on someone's face
Why does life hurt so much?
It doesn't have to be this way
It doesn't have to hurt, I say ..
where there is a will, there is a way

Try it, spread love today
to share our hope, instead of fear
just for this day, and
throughout the year
It doesn't have to hurt, I say
it doesn't have to be this way
a kind word
a gentle touch
something so easy, can give so much
expecting nothing in return
give it freely
try it, I say
life doesn't have to hurt this way

LET SOMEONE IN

When reality hurts and your
always in pain.
and you search your heart,
and you feel your insane.
When you close your eyes
and you try to sleep.
But some of the scars
go way to deep
to share who you are
to let someone in
All of your shame, all of your sin
When does it stop?
When does it end?
Can I learn not to break
maybe just bend.
When reality hurts, and
your always in pain

And you know that there
must be another way.
To share who you are
to let someone in.
The things you've done
the places you've been, and
each time we share
we lighten the load
and know we are on the recovery road
The hurts, and the pain
turn to love, and to hope
To realize there is a
life after dope.
When you share who you are,
and you let someone in
your future looks brighter
your new life begins
and to think it all starts
when you let someone in ...

I HAVE WORK TO DO

I'm sick and tired of being tired
I'm tired of being sick.
I can not talk, I can not speak
my tongue is way too thick.
I try to see, but I cannot
my pupils are but slits.
And when I think I know something
my brain, it is on E.
I tried to move my arms, but
then I noticed, they were wings.
So am I alive, or am I dead?
This, I do not know.
My lips are blue, and purple
and my skins as white as snow.
I take a walk, to look
to see if anyone is near.
I do not notice space, and time
and no one else is here.
I started to get frightened
and to my knees, I fell.
I cried out to my God
am I in heaven, or in hell?

He answered with a thunderous voice
He told me not to fear.
He said that He's not done with me
My time is not yet here.
Then my eyes were opened
and my heart was pumping blood.
And the love flowed right through me
like a wild, raging flood.
The room was full of people
and the light was way too bright
and they were all crying
because I died that night.
And when I took my first deep breath
they could not believe there eyes.
I told them to stop fussin
that I needed my shoes.
I told them what my God had said.
That I had work to do.
So now I have another life
a chance to do what's right.
How did this all happen?
I lost all my blood that night.
They say that its a miracle
there is no other way.
So now I devote my life to God
this day, and everyday ...

UNDERSTAND

What does it mean to understand?
To know without a doubt.
What does it mean to comprehend,
what life is all about?
To search for honesty, and for truth
to spread hope, and conquer fear
and not only listen, but
truly hear
to share love for others
and truly care
So, how do we begin to understand?
It starts within ourselves
when we open up, and share who we are
we let our love shine through.
Then we begin to understand
honesty and truth.
Then, we are on the right path
the narrow road, which leads to love
and we understand
that is what life truly is about ...

LIFE

Its not about how old you are,
its about the way you live ...
Its not about how much you have,
its about how much you give ...
Its not about standing proud, and tall,
but to learn to kneel, and bow ...
Its not about the future, or the past,
its about the here, and now ...
Its not about winning, or loosing,
or who is right, or wrong ...
Its more about relationships,
and how we get along ...
Its not about what you believe,
but do you practice, what you preach ...
Its not about how much you learned,
it about how much you teach ...
Its not about the clothes you wear,
its about what's deep inside ...
Its not about how long you lived,
but did you love before you died ...

CHAPTER 5

FAITH

Mark 5:34b

Thy faith hath made thee whole,
go in peace.

KJV

WHEN IT WAS WRITTEN

DOVE

When I think of you
I think of love
a pure, white precious dove

A gift from Him
from up above.

When I think of you
I think of happiness
joy, and, peace

When I think of you
I think of days gone by
and years to come

When I think of you
I think of love

A gift from Him
from up above.

WAIT

Sometimes its hard to wait
to learn to be patient, and calm
anxiety takes over
and I begin to worry
then, I remember God is in control ...
things happen in His time, not mine
and so I wait
and I learn
then I find peace in the fact
that God is in control ...
As the worry melts away
anxiety looses its grip
and I continue to learn
and I continue to wait
things happen as they should
when I wait
and remember, God is in control ...

HAPPY, JOYOUS, AND FREE

Let me tell you something
this thing happened to me
It wasn't overtime
it happened instantly
the wall around me crumbled
I'm happy, joyous, and free ...

I know it came from God
a pink cloud it may be
I may have heard it a hundred times
but for the first time, I can see
so let me keep it simple
its not a fantasy
this time, this is really real
I'm happy, joyous, and free ...

LOST

I could not find myself
I was lost without a trace ...

I could not find no love
I was lost in outer space ...

Now I'm asking you for help
please let me plead my case ...

And you tell me their is hope
that everything can change ...

Everything can change
when I join the human race ...

Now I have a choice to live
Its only through Gods grace ...

MERRY GO ROUND

I was on a merry go round
going round, and round
and I couldn't get off.
Going faster, out of control
afraid to jump, afraid to let go.
To make the change, to take it slow.
To give of myself, instead of receive
to ask for help, to get on my knees ..
to help someone else
to care for their needs.
Its that which I sow
Its that which I reap
gotta let go, gotta search deep.
Off the merry go round, onto my feet
then I can help others, that also helps me
to conquer my fears, to change what I see
I gotta jump, I gotta let go
I can not reap, unless I sow
to give of myself, instead of receive.
To reach out my hand, to help you believe
I have faith in God, its trust I need
to get off the merry go round, onto my feet ..

FAITH, HOPE & LOVE

Three small words –
Faith, hope & love

These I give to thee

Without them
their is nothing –

All goodness starts here
The opposite of anger & fear

Faith, hope & love

Three smalls words
that mean so much –

These I give to thee

Screams turn to whispers
pain turns to comfort

The best part of all
these gifts, their free

Faith, hope & love
these I give to thee –

CHAPTER 6

HOPE

Psalms 39:7

And now; Lord, what wait I for? My hope is in thee.

KJV

WHEN IT WAS WRITTEN

THE END OF A ROPE

I was hanging at the end of a rope
I was all alone, I had no hope
too much pain, I could not cope
Its getting tighter, now I choke
I closed my eyes, and said good-bye
But for some reason, the rope broke
And as I crashed onto the floor
A light shown through my open door
Its never been so bright before
An angel stood there, all aglow
He said, it's not my time to go
Then, I got up to my knees
I yelled out someone help me please
He said that He was there for me
To give me life, to help me see
To tell me that I'm not alone
To tell me that their still is hope

AS TWO WORLDS COLLIDE

I open my eyes, as two worlds collide
and pain and fear never subside
up the ladder, its time to climb
to tell the truth, to tell the lie
to choose to live, to choose to die
I close my eyes, as two worlds collide
and evil, and darkness deep inside
within myself, these things I hide
to search myself, to what I find
to cleanse my soul, to change my mind
I open my eyes as two worlds collide
And hope, and peace, can they be mine?
I pray to my God, to Him I confide
The days in the past, the times that I've tried
the battle within, the thing I must fight
there is always a choice, as two worlds collide ...

POWER

Thiers power in prayer
Thiers power in love
Thiers power in forgiveness
Thiers power in hope
Thiers power in wisdom
Thiers power in knowledge
Thiers power in letting go
Thiers power in acceptance
Thiers power in honesty
Thiers power in humility
Thiers power in unity
Thiers power in surrender

THE SOLUTION

Thier is a solution
as simple as it seems
If I do a little work
today, I can stay clean.

What is this solution?
Can it work for me?
All this time my eyes were closed
but now, I truly see.

As I live in the solution
I have new hope, new dreams
I see it working in your life
and I believe it can help me.

So now its time for action
this gift that I received
I didn't find the solution
Its the solution that found me ...

THE MESSAGE IS HOPE

The message is hope ...
The promise is freedom
Freedom from pain
Freedom from loneliness
Freedom from death

The message is love ...
The promise is freedom
Freedom from hatred
Freedom from aloneness
Freedom from self

The message is life ...
The promise is freedom
Freedom from disease
Freedom from addiction
Freedom from death

The message is hope ...

HOPE, FAITH, LOVE

I have so much hope
I have to give some away

I have so much faith
I have to give some way

I have so much love
I have to give some away

Hope, faith, and love
I have so much
that I must give some away

And in turn
I will receive even more
But I must give it away
in order to keep it.

I must give some away
if I want to receive it.

CHAPTER 7

I BECAME WE

Matthew 18:20

For where two, or three are gathered
together in My name, there am I
in the midst of them.

KJV

WHEN IT WAS WRITTEN

TOGETHER

Together we can do
What I can never do alone
I would not have made it this far
Without the kindness that you've shown
together we have comfort
together we have hope
I know I can't do it alone
but together we can cope
So what brought on this difference?
What brought on this change?
I finally made a decision
to no longer live in pain.
Now there is a solution
as simple as it seems
Together we can reach our goals
Our desires, and our dreams.
Through honesty, and trust
This foundation we have laid.
When I face a problem
or a decision must be made
I learn to pause a moment

I learn to stop and think
Together we are a strong chain
alone, I'm just a link.
Each day, I ask for help
our chain it grows in length
what I thought was weakness
now I see as strength.
Together we are stronger
together we can stand,
we are together, hand in hand.
So now I must move forward
thiers more that I can do
I cannot keep this to myself
I must share it with you.
I start each day
I thank God for another opportunity
together, its no longer, I
together, now its, We
together we are stronger
together we can stand
I know that I am not alone
we are together, hand in hand.

TAKE A RISK

When I come to another fork in the road
and I'm not sure which way to go
and I realize I may need some help
because I cannot do it by myself
to take a risk and trust in you
maybe your able to carry me through
and share with me your experience and hope
to show me a way, to help me to cope
what worked for you might work for me
as impossible as it may seem
to take a risk, to let you in
and you share with me where you've been
then I know that I'm not alone
together we are on the recovery road

I cannot do it without you
and then I learn, you need me to
as impossible as it may seem
together, we can beat this thing
when I take a risk, and open my heart
I begin to make a brand new start
when I open my heart, and I open my mind
and take a risk, there's love I find
and things get better over time
when I become more willing to try
To take a risk, to share my fears
and not be ashamed to show my tears
from all the pain, and all the years
and then I know that I'm not alone
and realize, its together we grow.

COME WITH ME

Come with me
I know a way to freedom today
I'll lead, you follow
maybe you'll lead tomorrow
we are on the path
the same path
that leads to freedom
come with me
I know the way to victory today
I'll lead, you follow
maybe you'll lead tomorrow
as long as we stay on the path
the same path.
Come with me.
I know the way.

YOU'RE RIGHT

You're right
I'll always be faithful, and true
no matter what I say, and do
why do I keep these words from you?
you're right
I'm afraid
Why? I have no clue
I see an angel, when I look at you
she spread her wings
away she flew
and left me alone
in the morning dew
you're right
I'll always be faithful, and true
no matter what happens
I'll always love you.
So why do I keep these words from you?
You deserve to hear them
yes its true
So always know
I love you
I do ...

LIKE A BOOK

If my mind was a book
and I opened it to you

Would you read a page?
Could you read a chapter?
If you could read my mind
and it read like a book
would you understand?

If my mind was a book
and I opened it to you

I could hide nothing from you
It would be open
For you to know all
Would you understand?
Could you separate fantasy from reality?
Would you see what was real?

If my mind was a book
and I opened it to you

Would you accept me?
If you knew all
Could you love me?
If you knew all

If my mind was a book
and I opened it to you

For you to know all
Would you love me?
If you knew all

Printed in the United States
by Baker & Taylor Publisher Services